FLAMINGOES

UNUSUAL ANIMALS

Lynn M. Stone

The Rourke Corporation, Inc.
Vero Beach, Florida 32964

Edited by Sandra A. Robinson

PHOTO CREDITS
All photos © Lynn M. Stone except page 15 © James P. Rowan;
page 17 © Joe McDonald.

ACKNOWLEDGMENTS
The author thanks Busch Gardens, Tampa, FL, for assistance in the
preparation of this book.

Library of Congress Cataloging-in-Publication Data

Stone, Lynn M.
   Flamingoes / by Lynn M. Stone.
   p.   cm. — (Unusual animals)
   Includes index.
   Summary: Discusses the physical characteristics, homes, and
behavior of this bird known for its colorful plumage, long legs, and
unusual bill.
   ISBN 0-86593-283-2
   1. Flamingos—Juvenile literature. [1. Flamingos.] — I. Title.
II. Series: Stone, Lynn M.   Unusual animals.
QL696.C56S76   1993
598.3'4—dc20
                                                    93-7587
                                                      CIP
                                                      AC
Printed in the USA

TABLE OF CONTENTS

THE UNUSUAL FLAMINGOES

The six **species,** or kinds, of flamingoes are remarkably unusual birds. Flamingoes show off lovely pink or reddish feathers, yet they are rather odd-looking creatures. They have the long necks and stiltlike legs of herons and storks. However, flamingoes sound—and often act—like geese.

Most long-legged wading birds have long, slender bills. The flamingo? It has a boxy bill—a one-of-a-kind creation.

As you might suspect, flamingoes begin life in unusual nests—"chimneys" of mud.

Pink feathers, a heavy bill and webbed feet make flamingoes different from other wading birds

HOW FLAMINGOES LOOK

Flamingoes are well-known for their bright **plumage,** or feathers. Their spindly legs and slender, S-curved necks are also eye-catching.

A flamingo at rest often stands on one leg. The "missing" leg is tucked beneath its body.

Flamingoes have webbed feet. Sometimes they paddle in deep water like geese.

Flamingoes stand up to 6 feet tall. In flight, flamingoes have a 5- to 6-foot **wingspan.**

One leg is as good as two for a Caribbean flamingo at rest

WHERE FLAMINGOES LIVE

The different species of flamingoes live in parts of western Asia, Africa, southern Europe, South America and southern North America.

Flamingoes live in some of the world's most rugged and out-of-the-way wetlands, from coastal swamps to salty lakes tucked away high in South American mountains.

The only wild flamingoes in North America are the Caribbean flamingoes. Their homes are on a few of the islands in the Caribbean Sea and in parts of northern South America.

Caribbean flamingoes live in Mexico and on a few Caribbean islands

WHAT FLAMINGOES EAT

The flamingo's remarkable bill is basically a curved, upside down bucket with a lid. Inside is a special strainer.

Flamingoes feed by pumping water and mud through their bills. The strainers filter food from the water and mud.

Flamingoes with extremely fine strainers eat plant life that is too small for us to see. Other flamingoes catch little water animals in their strainers.

Curiously, the only other animals that strain food as flamingoes do are some of the great whales. Other animals have "strainers," but don't use them as flamingoes and whales do.

Flamingoes dip their bills — and sometimes their heads — to feed

Oiling and cleaning feathers is part of this greater flamingo's daily workout

The Chilean flamingo is the smallest of three South American species

KINDS OF FLAMINGOES

The Caribbean flamingo is the rosiest flamingo species. The Caribbean flamingo and its closest cousin, the greater flamingo, are the world's largest flamingoes.

Lesser flamingoes are the most plentiful species. About 6 million of them live in Africa.

The Andean flamingo is the largest of the three South American flamingo species. The Chilean flamingo is the smallest. The "middle-sized" James' flamingoes live on high mountain lakes. They are the rarest flamingoes.

Lesser flamingoes flock by the thousands to Lake Nakuru in East Africa

FLAMINGO HABITS

Flamingoes are very **social.** They fly, nest, feed and rest together in large flocks. Some flocks of lesser flamingoes contain hundreds of thousands of birds. A nesting flock, or **colony,** in Kenya had more than 1 million nests!

Some flocks **migrate,** or travel, to new homes for part of the year.

As nesting time approaches, lovesick flamingoes hustle about. They call loudly to their mates as they flap their wings, run and jab at each other.

*Bird watching at its best —
flamingoes in graceful flight*

FLAMINGO NESTS

Many birds follow a nesting "schedule" each year. Flamingoes nest when the water level is low and plenty of mud is available.

Using their big bills, flamingoes shape solid "chimneys" of mud for their nests. Each nest stands about 1 foot tall. The flamingo lays a single white egg in a shallow "cup" on the "chimney" top.

Flamingo nests are close together, and the birds often squabble, jabbing at each other with their bills.

Remarkable flamingoes build remarkable "chimney" nests of mud

BABY FLAMINGOES

Adult flamingoes produce a bright red liquid in their throats after their young hatch. They dribble the liquid into the beaks of their babies. After 10 weeks of this liquid diet, a young flamingo can fly. Its pink, adult feathers are not fully in place, however, until it is four years old.

A baby flamingo may become **prey,** or food, for gulls, vultures, eagles, hogs and other animals. **Drought**—the lack of water—and floods are even greater threats.

This young flamingo will wait nearly four years for its rosy feathers

FLAMINGOES AND PEOPLE

Flamingoes are very fussy, or specialized, birds. Conditions have to be "just so" or they will not feed or nest.

Flamingoes have deserted many nesting and feeding sites because of people.

People have frightened flamingoes and sometimes collected their eggs. They have also destroyed flamingo **habitats,** or homes, by taking water away to cities.

However, people sometimes help flamingoes, too. Chile has a new refuge—a protected area that helps keep the three species of South American flamingoes safe.

Glossary

colony (KAHL uh nee) — a group of nesting animals of the same kind

drought (DROUT) — a long time without rain

habitat (HAB uh tat) — the kind of place in which an animal lives, such as a marshland

migrate (MY grate) — to move some distance from one place to another at the same time each year

plumage (PLOO mihdj) — the feathers on a bird

prey (PRAY) — an animal that is hunted for food by another animal

social (SO shul) — spending time in the company of others of the same kind

species (SPEE sheez) — within a group of closely-related animals, such as flamingoes, one certain kind or type (*Andean* flamingo)

wingspan (WING span) — the distance from the tip of one outstretched wing to the tip of the other

INDEX